Inside Out DAD®

Second Edition

FATHERING HANDBOOK

TO LEARN MORE ABOUT NFI AND THE *INSIDEOUT DAD*® PROGRAM AND PRODUCTS:

National Fatherhood Initiative®
www.fatherhood.org

TRAINING, TECHNICAL ASSISTANCE, AND QUESTIONS ABOUT THE INSIDEOUT DAD® PROGRAM

Phone: (301) 948-0599
Fax: (301) 948-6776
Email: info@fatherhood.org
Website: www.fatherhood.org

- www.fatherhood.org/the-father-factor
- www.facebook.com/nationalfatherhoodinitiative
- @thefatherfactor

LEARN MORE ABOUT NATIONAL FATHERHOOD INITIATIVE®

12410 Milestone Center Drive
Suite 600
Germantown, MD 20876

Phone: (301) 948-0599
Fax: (301) 948-6776
Email: info@fatherhood.org
Website: www.fatherhood.org

SECOND EDITION
Christopher Brown, (National Fatherhood Initiative®)
With contributions from Stephen Bavolek, Ph.D., CEO & Founder of Family Development Resources, Inc.;
Michael Yudt (National Fatherhood Initiative®)

© 2012, 2017 National Fatherhood Initiative®

Printed in the United States of America.

1567-06-2017-CNA-172

ATTENTION: Trademark and Copyright Protection
The manuals, inventories and other instructional materials published by National Fatherhood Initiative® are federally protected against unauthorized reproduction whether print or electronic.

TABLE OF CONTENTS

Session 1
Introduction: Getting Started 1

Session 2
Family History and The InsideOut Dad® 4

Session 3
What It Means to Be a Man 7

Session 4
Showing and Handling Feelings 11

Session 5
Men's Health 15

Session 6
Communication 19

Session 7
The Father's Role 26

Session 8
Children's Growth 33

Session 9
Discipline 37

Session 10
Working with Mom and Co-Parenting 45

Session 11
Fathering from the Inside 52

Session 12
Celebrate 59

Appendix
Ages and Stages 61

SESSION 1
Introduction: Getting Started

What Kind of Father and Partner Am I?
Father and Husband/Partner Checklist
Place a ✓ in the box if you **agree** with the statement about yourself as a Partner/Husband.

1. I listen to other points of view.
   ☐ Father   ☐ Husband/Partner

2. I can bargain and deal when needed.
   ☐ Father   ☐ Husband/Partner

3. I am clearly in charge.
   ☐ Father   ☐ Husband/Partner

4. I expect others to follow the rules I set down.
   ☐ Father   ☐ Husband/Partner

5. I demand respect.
   ☐ Father   ☐ Husband/Partner

6. I tell others what I think and feel in healthy ways.
   ☐ Father   ☐ Husband/Partner

7. I am willing to change my ideas.
   ☐ Father   ☐ Husband/Partner

8. I show a sense of closeness to those I love.
   ☐ Father   ☐ Husband/Partner

9. I like being in control.
   ☐ Father   ☐ Husband/Partner

10. I enjoy spending quality time with my family.
    ☐ Father   ☐ Husband/Partner

> Dads not only have traits and duties that have to do with being a dad, they also have traits and duties that have to do with their relationships with the mothers of their children.

SESSION 1 | Introduction: Getting Started

11. I am able to listen to the good as well as to the bad.
    ☐ Father   ☐ Husband/Partner

12. I am clearly seen as a friend.
    ☐ Father   ☐ Husband/Partner

13. Others can come to me to talk.
    ☐ Father   ☐ Husband/Partner

14. I am caring and giving.
    ☐ Father   ☐ Husband/Partner

15. I have fun easily.
    ☐ Father   ☐ Husband/Partner

My Story

The name of the actor starring in this movie is

_____.
(Your Name)

The story begins in _____.
(Place of Birth)

in the year _____.
(Date of Birth)

In the beginning, the major supporting actors in the story are

_____

_____.
(Childhood Family)

Today the major supporting actors are _____

_____

_____.
(Current Family)

This story is about a little boy who grows up believing _____

and then finds out in later life that _____

Introduction: Getting Started | **SESSION 1**

_____
_____.

There are many challenges in life faced by this boy and man, which include _____
_____ ,
but the most memorable scene takes place in _____
_____
when _____
_____ **happens.**

What makes this scene so memorable is _____
_____
_____.

Throughout life, the main character meets heroes like_____
_____
(People and/or Events)
and villains like _____
_____
_____.
(People and/or Events)

This ongoing story is heading toward _____
_____
_____.

And at the end of the story, the critics will say _____
_____
_____.

SESSION 2
Family History and The InsideOut Dad®

Welcome and Warm-Up
1. The most important trait of a father is _____.

2. The reason it is the most important trait is _____.

What it Means to be a Man and My Role
1. When I grew up, being a man meant that his role in the family was _____.

   (Yesterday's Father).

2. Today being a man to most guys I know means that his role in the family is _____.

   (Today's Father)

3. The way I see it, being a man means that my role in my family is _____.

   (My Role)

The InsideOut Dad®

1. **Self-Awareness.** The InsideOut Dad® is aware of himself as a man and aware of how important he is to his family. He knows his moods, feelings and emotions; capabilities, strengths, and challenges. He is responsible for his behavior and knows that his growth depends on how well he knows and accepts himself. He also knows that his ability to be with his children is affected by the choices he has made and accepts responsibility for his choices.

   The InsideOut Dad® asks himself: How well do I know myself?

2. **Caring for Self.** The InsideOut Dad® takes care of himself. He gets annual physicals, eats the right foods, works out to stay in shape, and learns about the world he lives in. He has a strong connection to his family and community, and chooses friends who support his healthy choices. While being locked up limits his choices, he takes every chance to keep himself physically and mentally fit so he can be the best example possible for his children.

   The InsideOut Dad® asks himself: How well do I care for myself?

3. **Fathering Skills.** The InsideOut Dad® knows his role in the family. He knows he is a model for his sons on how to be a good man and father and for his daughters on what they should look for in a husband and father for their children. The InsideOut Dad® uses his knowledge of the unique skills he and his wife/the mother of his children brings to raising his children. In other words, he knows the difference between "fathering" and "mothering."

   The InsideOut Dad® asks himself: How well do I "Father?"

4. **Parenting Skills.** The InsideOut Dad® nurtures his children. He knows how his parenting skills help to develop their physical, emotional, intellectual, social, spiritual, and creative needs. His children trust and feel safe with him because he cares about and nurtures them through the use of proven parenting skills. The InsideOut Dad® uses discipline to teach and guide his children, not to threaten or harm them.

SESSION 2 | Family History and The InsideOut Dad®

> The InsideOut Dad® knows his role in the family. He knows he is a model for his sons on how to be a good man and father and for his daughters on what they should look for in a husband and father for their children.

The InsideOut Dad® asks himself: How well do I "Parent?"

5. **Relationship Skills.** The InsideOut Dad® builds and maintains healthy relationships with his children, wife/mother of his children, other family members, friends, and community. He knows and values how relationships shape his children and their lives. The InsideOut Dad® knows how the relationship with his wife/mother of his children affects his children and does his best to create a good relationship with her for the sake of his children. He always looks to improve the skills he uses to communicate with others.

The InsideOut Dad® asks himself: How well do I relate?

What I Learned Log

1. One new thing I learned today is _____
   _____
   _____ .

2. On a scale from 0 - 5, how likely am I to use what I learned?
   0 = Not at all likely   5 = Very likely

       0   1   2   3   4   5

3. What I learned will help me be a better dad because: _____
   _____
   _____
   _____ .

Notes
_____
_____

SESSION 3
What It Means to Be a Man

Welcome and Warm-up

1. To me, being a man means _____
   _____
   _____ .

2. The trait of being a man I most admire is _____
   _____
   _____ .

3. The trait of being a man I least admire is _____
   _____
   _____ .

Today's Man

Think about the list of traits below that some people might use to define what it means to be a man.

- **Self-confident**
- **Courageous**
- **A Leader**
- **Dependable**
- **Successful**
- **Self-reliant**
- **Controlling (of situations or other people)**

On a scale from 0 - 3, rate yourself on the degree to which you have **those** traits. (Circle your answer.)

- **Self-confident:**

Not at all	A little	Average amount	A lot
0	1	2	3

SESSION 3 | What It Means to Be a Man

- **Courageous:**

Not at all	A little	Average amount	A lot
0	1	2	3

- **A Leader:**

Not at all	A little	Average amount	A lot
0	1	2	3

- **Dependable:**

Not at all	A little	Average amount	A lot
0	1	2	3

- **Successful:**

Not at all	A little	Average amount	A lot
0	1	2	3

- **Self-reliant:**

Not at all	A little	Average amount	A lot
0	1	2	3

- **Controlling (of situations or other people):**

Not at all	A little	Average amount	A lot
0	1	2	3

2. **Today**
   Write up to 7 traits that best describe what it means to be a man **today**. Use what you and the other Dads already said or just your thoughts, then circle your answer.

   1. _____

Not at all	A little	Average amount	A lot
0	1	2	3

   2. _____

Not at all	A little	Average amount	A lot
0	1	2	3

What It Means to Be a Man | **SESSION 3**

3. _____

Not at all	A little	Average amount	A lot
0	1	2	3

4. _____

Not at all	A little	Average amount	A lot
0	1	2	3

5. _____

Not at all	A little	Average amount	A lot
0	1	2	3

6. _____

Not at all	A little	Average amount	A lot
0	1	2	3

7. _____

Not at all	A little	Average amount	A lot
0	1	2	3

3. **Traits to Pass on to My Children**
   Write up to 7 traits you would like to pass on to your son(s) or to model for your daughter(s).

   1. _____

   2. _____

   3. _____

   4. _____

   5. _____

   6. _____

   7. _____

SESSION 3 | What It Means to Be a Man

> Although our culture doesn't "objectify" men as much as it does women, it still sends unreal images and messages about the link between what men should look like and how that defines a man.

Body Image

1. Examples of working out include _____ , _____ , _____ , and _____ .

2. "Body image" means _____ .

3. Although our culture doesn't "objectify" men as much as it does women, it still sends unreal images and messages about the link between what men should look like and how that defines a man.

4. Being an InsideOut Dad® means that as a man you take care of your health. Letting yourself go isn't manly and isn't part of being an InsideOut Dad®.

What I Learned Log

1. One new thing I learned today is _____ .

2. On a scale from 0 - 5, how likely am I to use what I learned?

   0 = Not at all likely   5 = Very likely

   0   1   2   3   4   5

3. What I learned will help me be a better dad because: _____ .

SESSION 4
Showing and Handling Feelings

> It is how the energy shows itself that gets people into trouble.

Welcome and Warm-up
1. I was told when I was a boy that showing my feelings or emotions was _____.

2. Today I feel that it is _____ to show my feelings or emotions.

Holding Feelings Inside
1. One feeling I have trouble handling is _____
   _____.

2. When I feel _____,
   I usually _____.

3. It's okay in some cases to not show your feelings or emotions. When you face danger, for example, it's okay to not show fear when fear might keep you from taking action. Men tend to better control their feelings than women. Because men and women process feelings differently, dads don't deal with their feelings in exactly the same ways as moms do.

4. All feelings are okay. They're neither good nor bad, they're just feelings. It is the way that we show and handle our feelings that can cause problems.

5. Thoughts and feelings have energy. It is the energy that wants to show itself. There are right or respectful and wrong or disrespectful ways to show the

SESSION 4 | Showing and Handling Feelings

> Thoughts and feelings have energy. It is the energy that wants to show itself. There are right or respectful and wrong or disrespectful ways to show the energy of thoughts and feelings.

energy of thoughts and feelings. The InsideOut Dad® follows the rules below when he shows and handles his thoughts and feelings.

Respect Yourself: Don't disrespect yourself.
Respect Others: Don't disrespect others.
Respect the Earth: Don't disrespect the Earth.

Grief and Loss

1. Loss means to not have something any longer; to have something taken away by accident, carelessness, parting, or death.

2. You can lose things you can see, such as money, home, a parent or child, or a job. You can also lose things you can't see, such as love, health, respect, and self-worth.

3. Grief is how people react to loss. How people react differs with the kind of loss, what the loss meant to them, how much loss they've had in their lives, and how they handle loss.

4. Men tend to:
   - Not take care of their emotions when they grieve. They hide their grief. They say things like, "It doesn't hurt that bad" or "I'm okay" to keep people away.
   - Take time away or want to be alone to think things through.
   - Show anger more often than sadness.
   - Grieve through rituals, such as doing or making something.

5. Tips for how to grieve:
   - Show courage. Allow yourself to grieve. Don't hide your feelings.
   - Tell people when you need to be alone to think things through.
   - Don't shut others out.
   - Listen to your body and become aware of how your body reacts

to grief. For example, do you get sick to your stomach or get a headache?

- Use rituals and activity to work through your grief.
- Slow down and reflect on the cause of your grief.
- Stay close to friends you can count on.
- Stay in good health and work out.
- Cry if you need to.

6. One message I got about crying was _____
   _____
   _____ .

7. The message I send to my children about crying is _____
   _____
   _____ .

8. The biggest loss that I never grieved is _____
   _____
   _____ .

What I Learned Log

1. One new thing I learned today is _____
   _____
   _____ .

2. On a scale from 0 - 5, how likely am I to use what I learned?
   0 = Not at all likely   5 = Very likely

       0   1   2   3   4   5

3. What I learned will help me be a better dad because: _____
   _____
   _____ .

SESSION 4 | Showing and Handling Feelings

> Listen to your body and become aware of how your body reacts to grief. For example, do you get sick to your stomach or get a headache?

Notes

SESSION 5
Men's Health

Welcome and Warm-up

1. On a scale from 1 to 5, with 1 being very low and 5 being very high, I rate how I take care of my physical health as a _____ .

2. On a scale from 1 to 5, with 1 being very low and 5 being very high, I rate how I take care of my mental health as a _____ .

3. One thing I can do to improve my physical health is _____
   _____
   _____ .

4. One thing I can do to improve my mental health is _____
   _____
   _____ .

Stress and Anger

1. Mental health is the ability to adjust to and meet the demands of everyday life. "Good" mental health means the ability to think things through so that you can adjust to and meet the demands in your life in ways that don't harm you or others.

2. Mental health affects your physical health and your physical health affects your mental health. If you have a problem with your mental health, it will show up in your body. If you have a problem with the health of your body, it will affect your mind and how you see the world.

Drinking and Stress

1. **Stress and Alcohol Quiz:**

   1) **Drinking alcohol reduces your stress.**
      Myth and Fact. Alcohol in very small amounts may lower the body's response to stress. But alcohol, especially in large amounts, actually increases the stress response by causing the body to release

> Your body will be affected if you have a problem with your mental health. Likewise, your mind, and how you see the world, will be affected if your body isn't healthy.

SESSION 5 | Men's Health

> What often happens is men ignore the signs for so long that by the time they go to the doctor, it's too late.

the same hormones, such as adrenaline, that it produces under stress.

2) **Stress causes alcoholism.**
   Myth. Stress does not cause alcoholism, but problem drinking does increase stress.

3) **People don't know when they are addicted to alcohol.**
   Myth. People have symptoms that show they have a drinking problem. Common symptoms include heavy drinking after a fight with your wife or partner, when your boss gives you a difficult time, when you feel under pressure, drinking a lot when you're alone, and hiding how much you drink.

4) **You can inherit alcoholism.**
   Fact. Alcoholism runs in families. But not all children of alcoholics become alcoholic, and some people become alcoholics even though no one in their family is one.

5) **Alcoholism can be cured.**
   Myth. Alcoholism cannot be cured. Even if an alcoholic hasn't drunk for a long time, he can suffer a relapse. To guard against a relapse, an alcoholic must avoid any alcohol.

6) **Women shouldn't drink when they are pregnant.**
   Fact. Drinking while pregnant is dangerous. It can damage the brain and facial features of a baby while still in the womb. Alcohol use can also lower a man's sperm count, which can lead to problems in trying to have children.

More on Stress and Anger

1. When a feeling is not allowed to show itself, it is like stepping on a spring. When the pressure is off, feelings spring out. Feelings and thoughts have energy. It is how the energy shows itself that gets people into trouble.

2. The way I show my anger is _____
   _____.

3. I learned this way from _____
   _____.

Men's Health | **SESSION 5**

4. One way my children show their anger is _____
   _____
   _____ .

5. They learned this way from _____
   _____
   _____ .

6. Use the same rules of the InsideOut Dad® you learned during the last session to show your anger in healthy ways.

   Respect Yourself: **Don't disrespect yourself.**
   Respect Others: **Don't disrespect others.**
   Respect the Earth: **Don't disrespect the Earth.**

Physical Health

1. Men are raised to bury and ignore their physical problems. They're taught that their bodies should be able to "take a licking and keeping on ticking" which leads men to abuse their bodies and ignore warning signs that tell them they need help. What often happens is men ignore the signs for so long that by the time they go to the doctor, it's too late.

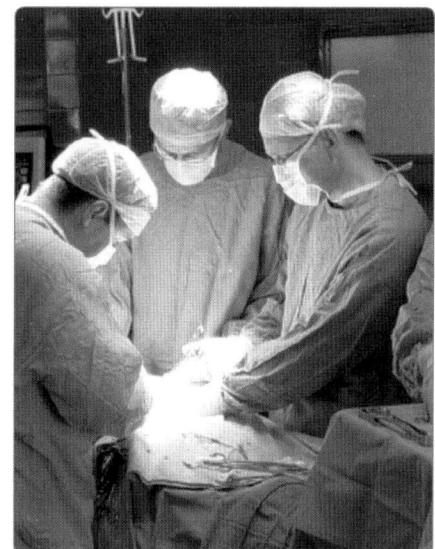

2. The part of my physical health that I am most concerned about is _____
   _____ .

3. I need to _____
   _____
   to take better care of my physical and mental health.

SESSION 5 | Men's Health

What I Learned Log

1. One new thing I learned today is _____
   _____
   _____ .

2. On a scale from 0 - 5, how likely am I to use what I learned?
   0 = Not at all likely   5 = Very likely

   0   1   2   3   4   5

3. What I learned will help me be a better dad because: _____
   _____
   _____ .

Notes

_____
_____
_____
_____
_____
_____
_____
_____
_____
_____

SESSION 6
Communication

> The InsideOut Dad® understands that problems with communication start with him and no one else.

Welcome and Warm-up

1. My strongest area of communication is _____
   _____
   _____ .

2. My weakest area of communication is _____
   _____
   _____ .

3. What I need to learn is _____
   _____
   _____ .

Ways of Communicating

1. The InsideOut Dad® communicates his thoughts, feelings, and actions on a daily basis in a way that respects others. He understands that problems with communication start with him and no one else.

2. **Fight or Flight Posture:**
   - **Blame Others/Get Angry**
     Mom: You need to be a better father.
     Dad: Well if you weren't such a bad mom, maybe I'd be a better father.

   - **Dismiss**
     Mom: You need to get a better job.
     Dad: You don't know what you're talking about. I have a good job.

   - **Start a Fight**
     Mom: Stop being so lazy.
     Dad: Look who's talking— you're the laziest person I know.

SESSION 6 | Communication

- **Check Out**
  Mom: Get a life.
  Dad: I don't have to listen to this. I'm going to watch TV.

3. **Defensive or Closed Posture:**
   - **Withdraw**
     Mom: You need to be a better father.
     Dad: (With arms crossed) Sits down and looks at his feet.

   - **Stubborn**
     Mom: You need to get a better job.
     Dad: (With arms crossed) I like my job. It's great, and I don't plan to get another one.

   - **Silent Treatment or The Look**
     Mom: Stop being so lazy.
     Dad: (With arms crossed) Doesn't say anything or gives an angry stare.

   - **Deny**
     Mom: Get a life.
     Dad: I've got a life. No problems here.

   - **Excuses**
     Mom: Why didn't you pick up your son/daughter today when you knew he/she was counting on you! That's the second time this month!
     Dad: I had something more important to do.

4. **Open for Change Posture:**
   - **Makes Eye Contact**
     Mom: You need to be a better father.
     Dad: (With arms held relaxed by his side) Makes eye contact with facilitator and has pleasant look on his face.

   - **Asks Questions Nicely**
     Mom: You need to get a better job.
     Dad: (With arms relaxed by his side) What kind of job do you think I should get?

- **Tries to Understand**
  Mom: Stop being so lazy.
  Dad: (With arms relaxed by his side) I don't understand. Why do you think I'm lazy?

- **Seeks Clarity**
  Mom: Get a life.
  Dad: (With arms relaxed by his side) I hear you saying I don't have a life. Is that my entire life or just a part of it?

5. With the mother of my children, I am most often in this posture (circle your answer):

   Fight or Flight   Defensive/Closed   Open for Change

   I am most often in this posture with her because_____
   _____
   _____ .

6. With my children, I am most often in this posture (circle your answer):

   Fight or Flight   Defensive/Closed   Open for Change

   I am most often in this posture with them because _____
   _____
   _____ .

7. With my friends, I am most often in this posture (circle your answer):

   Fight or Flight   Defensive/Closed   Open for Change

   I am most often in this posture with them because _____
   _____
   _____ .

> If you don't believe you need to change anything, you won't make the effort to listen to the need for change.

8. **Tips to be more "Open for Change":**

   - **Value the need to change and listen.** The InsideOut Dad® understands that problems with communication start with him and no one else. If you don't believe you need to change anything, you won't make the effort to listen to the need for change.

   - **Value the other person.** If you don't believe that someone else might have a point, you won't listen to what they have to say about a change you need to make. You'll see them as nagging you.

   - **Be aware of your usual posture or response to change.** The InsideOut Dad® is self-aware.

   - **Be aware of the mood of the other person.** How you respond depends in part on how angry or nice the other person is at the time. If she's angry, she'll be less likely to hear you and will tend to react much worse to your response.

   - **Be aware of your surroundings.** Who else is within ear shot? Are you in a public place? Does the other person have someone around (like a 6 foot, 4 inch 230-pound brother) who might get angry if you get into a Fight or Flight Posture?

   - **Use the skills you'll learn in this program.** You'll learn how to listen and talk in healthy ways. If you don't use them or use them well, you'll have a harder time with people.

Talking with Children

1. **Honor What They Want.**
   Children want things or want to do things right away. They don't like to wait. Tell them you hear what they want and that you know it's important to them. Hearing what someone says honors them. This doesn't mean that you give in, only that you hear them. Check in to make sure you know what they want and then respond. Hearing what

Communication | **SESSION 6**

they want will "soften the blow" if you tell them they can't have it, do it at all, or that they'll have to wait longer for what they want.

2. **Send Good Messages to Yourself.**
Children sometimes send themselves bad messages, such as they're no good, they're not smart, they're too short or too tall. They hear these messages from friends, parents, TV, and the Internet. Teach your children to send good messages to themselves, such as "I'm smart," "I'm going to do well on this test," "I can become anything I want to become." This is a skill that will last a lifetime.

3. **Avoid Bad Labels.**
Don't give your children a bad label based on what they want, say, or do. Dads often label what their children want, say, or do as bad, lazy, dumb, and crazy. Worse, Dads often label their children as bad, lazy, dumb, and spoiled to describe their children as a whole. Bad labels only create more of what you don't want to see. When your children want, say, or do something you don't agree with, don't put a label on it. Don't say, "That's dumb to want a bike right now." Instead say, "I hear that you want a bike right now, but I just don't have the money to pay for it. Maybe in a few months." Good labels will create more of what you want to see. Labels such as good, smart, special, and caring will go a long way toward helping you and your child enjoy your talks.

4. **Focus on the Goal.**
This is a no-brainer for Dads. Men know how to see a goal and what to do to get there. We know how

> Bad labels only create more of what you don't want to see. When your children want, say, or do something you don't agree with, avoid putting a label on it.

to take action to solve a problem. Ask your children to describe their goals in life and for certain things. Ask them, "What is your goal?" Then help them think through the actions they can take to get there.

5. **Focus on What They Learn.**
This isn't as easy for Dads. Dads often yell at or tear down their children after their children do something wrong. They point out what their children did wrong again and again without saying what their children did right. This approach doesn't help children

learn from their mistakes. All children hear is the yelling and the bad labels instead of seeing the lessons. When your children do something wrong, ask, "What did you learn?" or "What would you do instead the next time?" If your children don't see the lessons, point them out after you give them a chance to say what they learned. This approach honors your children and makes it more likely they'll listen to your wisdom. Besides, you might be surprised at how much your children say they learn from their mistakes. Use this tip not only when your children do something wrong, use it when they do something right. Perhaps they can do even better the next time.

What I Learned Log

1. One new thing I learned today is _____
_____
_____
_____
_____.

2. On a scale from 0 - 5, how likely am I to use what I learned?

   0 = Not at all likely   5 = Very likely

       0   1   2   3   4   5

3. What I learned will help me be a better dad because: _____

   _____

   _____

   _____.

Notes

SESSION 7 | The Father's Role

SESSION 7
The Father's Role

Welcome and Warm-up

1. One memory I have of my father (or father figure) is _____
   _____
   _____ .

2. What is unique about this memory is _____
   _____
   _____ .

The Ideal Father

1. **Traits** of the Ideal Father: What does the ideal father have?

   _____
   _____
   _____
   _____
   _____
   _____

2. **Duties** of the Ideal Father: What is the role of the ideal father?

   _____
   _____
   _____
   _____
   _____
   _____

Competitive and Non-Competitive Fathering

1. Competitive vs. Non-competitive Fathering Survey

    Put a check mark by the characteristic that is "more like me" in each of the following categories.

    1) Sports
        - ☐ a. Win at all costs
        - ☐ b. Have fun; improve skills

    2) Grades
        - ☐ a. Straight As
        - ☐ b. Study hard; do the best you can

    3) Achievement
        - ☐ a. Never be satisfied
        - ☐ b. Take pride in accomplishment and pride in yourself for your efforts

    4) Possessions
        - ☐ a. Bigger, better, faster, more expensive
        - ☐ b. Functional, useful, practical

    5) Parenting
        - ☐ a. Always right; authoritative
        - ☐ b. Democratic

    6) Relationships
        - ☐ a. Need to be in control
        - ☐ b. Shares control

    7) Efforts
        - ☐ a. More outcomes oriented
        - ☐ b. More process oriented

    8) Career
        - ☐ a. Strives to move up at the expense of job satisfaction and family time
        - ☐ b. Advancement not as important as job satisfaction and time with family

SESSION 7 | The Father's Role

> Children who grow up with their married parents are, for example, less likely to be abused and to misbehave in or drop out of school.

2. Competition in and of itself is not a bad thing, but it can harm fathers, their children, and others when they bring competition into their fathering to such a degree that it determines how they father on a daily basis. The point is not to "go easy" on your children, but to father them with a balance between competitive and non-competitive approaches and to know when they cross the line.

Benefits of Marriage

1. One benefit of marriage is

   _____

   because _____

   _____

   _____ .

2. The 7 Benefits of Marriage for Men:
   1) **Healthy Children**
      Children who grow up in a home with their two married parents are healthier, on average, than children who grow up in a home in which their parents just live together. Children who grow up with their married parents are, for example, less likely to be abused and to misbehave in or drop out of school. These children are more likely to have good marriages of their own. They are also less likely to face teen pregnancy and

drug or alcohol abuse. Marriage gives children the best chance at a healthy life!

2) **Healthy Marriages Lead to Strong Relationships With Children**
Marriage provides the best chance for fathers to create strong relationships with their children. Men who wait to have kids until they marry are three times more likely to be involved in their children's lives than are men who have kids outside of marriage. Dads who have good marriages are, on average, more involved in their children's lives than are never-married or divorced dads. That's because it's easier for married men to be with their children every day, and to nurture their kids at every stage of growth. Marriage can provide the joy of growing with your children every day!

3) **Better Family Finances**
Married couples have twice the money and assets that unmarried couples do. This can create a better financial future for couples and their children. Married men are also more likely to save and invest, even when they have the same income as unmarried men. Marriage also comes with tax, inheritance, and Social Security benefits. Marriage can help you make the most of your family's finances!

4) **Fuller, Happier Lives**

Married men are more likely to say they are happy than are unmarried men. After divorce, men are worse off overall than are women. The well-being of the family is the highest priority for most married men. When men focus on their wives and their children, not just on themselves, it helps them to lead full, happy lives. Married men are also less likely to be depressed. Marriage gives men more family members they can turn to for social, emotional, and financial support. Marriage can benefit you through a focus on the family!

> Married men are more than twice as likely to say they are happy than are unmarried men.

> On average, married men live longer than do unmarried men.

5) **A Long, Healthy Life**
A full, happy life often leads to a long, healthy life. On average, married men live longer than do unmarried men. Married men are more likely to take care of themselves. For example, they're more likely to stay in shape and to get medical help when they need it. Married men are less likely to do things that can hurt them, such as smoking, drinking, or using illegal drugs. Marriage can give you a great chance at a long, healthy life!

6) **More, Better, and Safer Sex**
One sign of a full, happy life is an active, good, and safe sex life. Married couples say they have sex more often than do unmarried people. Married men say they have better sex than do unmarried men. Married men work hard to build healthy relationships with their wives. They know that sex is best when they stay faithful to one woman. They also know that sex is best when they are emotionally close to their wives. When a husband and a wife are faithful, sex is safer physically and emotionally. There is little chance that you will get a sexual disease if you and your wife are faithful. Marriage can give you the best chance for an active, great, and safe sex life!

7) **Increased Faithfulness**
One reason that sex is better and safer in marriage is that married men and women are, on average, more faithful to each other than are men and women who simply live together or who date. You may be surprised to learn that most married men and women are faithful to each other. One study found that only 4 percent of wives are unfaithful compared to 20 percent of unmarried women who live with a man and 18 percent of women who date. Marriage can reduce the chance that the woman you love will cheat on you!

What I Learned Log

1. One new thing I learned today is _____

   _____

   _____

   _____ .

2. On a scale from 0 - 5, how likely am I to use what I learned?

   0 = Not at all likely   5 = Very likely

      0   1   2   3   4   5

3. What I learned will help me be a better dad because: _____

   _____

   _____

   _____ .

Notes

SESSION 8
Children's Growth

> Children who have high self-worth think and feel that they are good people and that they are worthy of love from others and themselves.

Welcome and Warm-up

1. One goal that my parents had for me that I was able to achieve was _____.

2. When I met this goal I felt _____.

3. One goal my parents had for me that I didn't achieve was _____.

4. When I didn't meet this goal I felt _____.

Goals and Self-Worth

1. **Self-worth** is the overall value people have for themselves. Self-worth combines people's self-concept (thoughts about themselves) and self-esteem (feelings about themselves).

Children's Growth | **SESSION 8**

2. When a child doesn't meet the goals their Dad has for them, what likely happens to their self-worth?

_____
_____
_____
_____
_____.

3. When a child meets the goals their Dad has for them, what likely happens to their self-worth? _____
_____
_____.

4. Children's self-worth not only changes based on whether they meet their Dad's goals, but they learn to anticipate their Dad's goals and how he'll react when they meet or don't meet them based on the patterns their Dad sets. Sadly, many Dads set the bar too high and their children are never able to reach their Dad's goals. It's okay and good for Dads to have goals for their children and to tell their children about the goals. What harms children is when the goals aren't realistic and Dads react poorly when their children don't reach them.

> It's okay and good for Dads to have goals for their children and to tell their children about the goals. What harms children is when the goals aren't realistic and Dads react poorly when their children don't reach them.

SESSION 8 | Children's Growth

> Today it's generally known that people are the way they are largely because of both forces—nature and nurture.

Nature or Nurture?

1. **Nature** is the traits that a person is born with and that don't change, such as race, sex, and hair and eye color. These are traits that parents can't affect.

2. **Nurture** is the way parents raise and treat their children. Nurture affects some traits, such as self-worth, how a child treats others, and what a child does for a job as an adult.

3. The way parents raise children can strengthen a natural weakness or weaken a natural strength. Parents can bring out and grow or suppress and not develop children's natural talents. At the same time, parents can get their children training to run faster, but their children can only run as fast as their natural gifts will allow. Parents can make sure their children eat the most healthy foods to grow taller, but their children will only grow as tall as their bodies will let them.

4. How to Use the Ages and Stages Charts:
   - **These charts can worry some Dads.** Don't let them scare you. They can be helpful. The fact is there is too much to know about children's growth without looking to the charts for help. Even pediatricians (doctors for children) keep these kinds of charts to refer to in their work!

   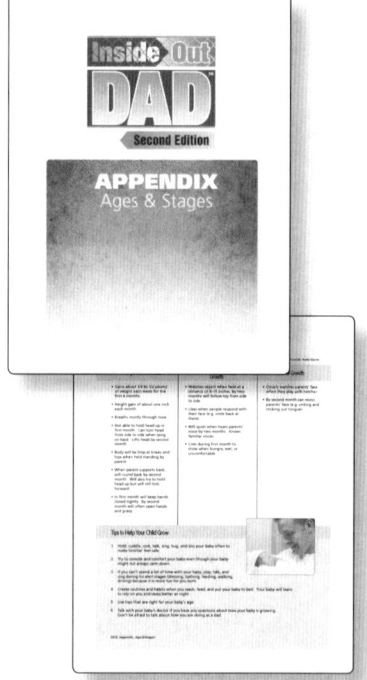

   - **Don't use the charts like report cards.** Don't compare your children to other children or your children to each other. The charts are only road maps to guide you on what most children should be able to do at a certain age.

   All children grow at different rates. The main thing is that your children are able to do these things at some point even if at a later age. If you are ever worried about how your child is growing, talk with your child's doctor.

5. Three things I can do right away to help my child to grow healthy and strong are:

   1) _____

   2) _____

   3) _____

What I Learned Log

1. One new thing I learned today is _____.

2. On a scale from 0 - 5, how likely am I to use what I learned?

   0 = Not at all likely   5 = Very likely

      0   1   2   3   4   5

SESSION 8 | Children's Growth

3. What I learned will help me be a better dad because: _____

_____

_____

_____

_____.

Notes

SESSION 9
Discipline

> Discipline comes from the Latin word "discipulus" meaning "to teach; to guide."

Welcome and Warm-up

1. One time that sticks out in my mind when my father or mother disciplined me was _____ .

2. What I learned from that discipline was _____ .

Morals and Values

1. **Discipline** comes from the Latin word "discipulus" meaning "to teach; to guide."

2. **Morals** are the rules for and habits of good or right behavior. They tell us what is right and wrong.

3. One moral I learned in childhood that I still practice today is _____

   because _____ .

4. One moral I learned in childhood that I don't practice today is _____

   because _____ .

SESSION 9 | Discipline

> Modeling is one of the most important ways that parents teach morals and values because they can model them on purpose and not on purpose.

5. One moral I teach my children that they practice is_____

   because _____

   _____ .

6. **Values** are what someone thinks is important or that has worth.

7. **Modeling** is one of the most important ways that parents teach morals and values because they can model them on purpose and not on purpose. Dads who say one thing but do another confuse their children because they don't "walk the talk." The role model they present doesn't place value on the moral because they say one thing and do another.

8. Styles of Discipline:
   - **Style #1: Dictator.** This Dad is always strict and never nurtures. He's clear about his morals and values. He leads with control and enforces rules with an iron hand. His children know what he doesn't want them to do but rarely what he wants them to do. This Dad says, "My way or the highway."
   - **Style #2: King.** This Dad is strict and nurtures when needed. He is clear about his morals and values. He leads by example. His children know what he doesn't want them to do and what he wants them to do. This Dad says, "Let me show you the way."
   - **Style #3 Joker.** This Dad is never strict and rarely nurtures. He isn't clear about his morals and values. He jokes a lot and makes fun of his children. His children don't know what he doesn't want them to do or what he wants them to do. This Dad says, "Let's just have fun."
   - **Style #4: Follower.** This Dad is sometimes strict and sometimes nurtures. He lets Mom take the lead on discipline and backs her up when needed. He is sometimes clear about his morals and values. His children know some of

the things he doesn't want them to do and some of the things he does want them to do. This Dad says, "Do whatever Mom says."

- **Style #5: Dreamer.** This Dad is never strict and never nurtures. He lets Mom take the lead on discipline and doesn't get involved with it. He is never clear about his morals and values. His children don't know what he wants them to do. This Dad says, "Whatever. Just leave me alone."

9. My style of discipline is _____.

10. I use this style because _____.

11. With my style of discipline, I want to make sure my children learn _____.

12. What I'm afraid they might be learning is _____.

SESSION 9 | Discipline

My Discipline from My Children's Point of View

Discipline | **SESSION 9**

Rewards and Punishment

1. Many Dads believe that discipline means "to control" rather than "to teach or to guide." As a result, they use fear when they punish.

2. Tips to Make Sure You Teach and Guide:
   - **Don't Rely on Shame and Blame.** Don't tell your children they're "no good" or "bad." Avoid shame and blame. When you use them children learn that **they**, instead of their actions, are not okay.

   - **Focus on the "Action" not the "Actor."** Talk about what your child did. It's okay, for example, to say that your child did something "bad" as long as you don't say your child is "bad" for doing it. Keep the focus on the action.

   - **Repair the Hurt.** Children can view discipline as hurtful. Repair the hurt by telling them that you love them no matter what and just because of who they are, even when they do something wrong and you have to discipline or punish them.

3. Discipline has to be clear, consistent, and doable. To achieve this goal, every rule needs a consequence so children learn the basic idea of discipline. A simple statement is "If-Then" as in, "If you do

   _____ ,

   then _____

   _____

   will happen." The If-Then statement helps children learn to make good choices.

4. Many Dads define discipline as punishment. In other words, they don't see punishment as a way to discipline in certain situations. They see punishment and discipline as the same thing. **Discipline means**

> Many Dads believe that discipline means "to control" rather than "to teach or to guide." As a result, they use fear when they punish.

SESSION 9 | Discipline

> Discipline means to teach or guide. Punishment means to "penalize" for doing something wrong.

to teach or guide. Punishment means to "penalize" for doing something wrong.

6. Tips to Reward Children

- **Praise:** Tell your child how much you like correct behavior and that your child is a good person for doing it.

- **Touch:** Give your child a hug, gentle pat on the back, or high five.

- **Freedoms:** Give your child a new freedom, such as to stay out later or read an extra story at bedtime.

- **Presents:** Give your child a toy, stickers, a new phone, or some extra cash. Focus on something they highly value.

Note: Use freedoms and presents sparingly. Make sure you <u>will</u> be able to give a freedom or present before offering one. Don't say you'll give one for correct behavior and then not give it when your child does the behavior.

7. Tips to Punish Children:

- **Say You're Disappointed:** Tell your children you expect more of them, and that you expect them to behave the right way.

- **Pay it Back:** Tell your child to make up for bad behavior, such as paying for breaking something, doing the behavior they were supposed to do in the first place, or saying they're sorry to someone they hurt.

Discipline | **SESSION 9**

- **Time Out:** Tell your child to sit in a safe place like a corner, on the couch, or go to their room for a short period of time. Time out works best with younger children between the ages of 3 and 10. A basic rule is 1 minute for every year of your child's age. But if you think your child has learned a lesson with a shorter period of time, don't require your child to sit in time out longer than needed. Use time outs to help your child regain control of himself/herself—such as when your child throws a tantrum—more than for other reasons. Your child only needs to stay in time out until your child regains control.

- **Grounding:** Don't let your child leave the house for some period of time. Grounding works best with older children, such as teens.

- **Take Away a Freedom:** Remove a freedom for a period of time.

Note: Make sure the punishment fits the problem behavior. Don't take away a freedom, for example, when a child does something minor when simply telling them that you expect more of them the next time will do the trick. Don't overuse any of these tips because children can become so used to them that they no longer have the desired effect.

> Make sure the punishment fits the problem behavior. Don't take away a freedom, for example, when a child does something minor when simply telling them that you expect more of them the next time will do the trick.

What I Learned Log

1. One new thing I learned today is _____
   _____
   _____ .

2. On a scale from 0 - 5, how likely am I to use what I learned?
   0 = Not at all likely   5 = Very likely

      0   1   2   3   4   5

3. What I learned will help me be a better dad because: _____
   _____
   _____ .

SESSION 9 | Discipline

Notes

SESSION 10
Working with Mom and Co-Parenting

Welcome and Warm-up

1. The main issues my children's mother and I have in raising our children together are _____
   _____
   _____
   _____.

2. The ways these issues affect our children are _____
   _____
   _____
   _____.

Parenting Differences

1. Although differences in parenting styles can create issues between parents, what causes **major** problems are differences in overall parenting approaches. An approach is a way to go about doing a task or solving a problemes. When parents have a different way to go about being parents, it creates problems.

2. Beliefs, morals, and values lead to different approaches. Values are the things people think are important and have worth. If parents believe that different things are important and have worth, it's easy to see how their approaches can lead to problems.

> Although differences in parenting styles can create issues between parents, what causes **major** problems are differences in overall parenting approaches.

> **IMPORTANT POINT**
> Parents can have different styles of parenting but the same underlying beliefs, morals, and values about parenting. What creates different parenting approaches are differences in beliefs, morals, and values about parenting.

> Beliefs, morals, and values lead to different approaches.

3. **Differences I Can Solve:**

   1) _____
   _____
   _____

   How to solve it: _____
   _____
   _____
   _____

   2) _____
   _____
   _____

   How to solve it: _____
   _____
   _____
   _____

   3) _____
   _____
   _____

   How to solve it: _____
   _____
   _____
   _____

4. **Value the need to change and listen.** If you don't believe you need to change anything, you won't make the effort to listen to the need for change.

5. **Value the other person.** If you don't believe that someone else might have a point, you won't listen to what the person has to say about a change you need to make. You'll see the person as nagging you.

Tips to Solve Parenting Differences

1. **Get in touch with your point of view.** Ask yourself: Where did it come from? What caused it? Why do I defend it? What am I holding on to?

2. **Listen to Mom's point of view.** Ask her: Where does it come from? Why do you believe or value it?

3. **Know that Mom's view is as important to her as yours is to you.**

4. **Put yourself in Mom's shoes to see things as she does.**

5. **Use these ground rules:**
   - No more than 15 to 30 minutes for talking.
   - Don't shout or yell at her.
   - No name calling.
   - Stick to the subject or difference.
   - Don't bring up the past if it has nothing to do with the difference.
   - Keep calm and end the talk if one of you becomes angry.
   - Respect each other.

6. Be willing to bargain or strike a deal. What can each of you give to the other? What is each of you willing to let go of?

7. Be ready to walk away if you or she becomes angry.

8. It might take more than one talk to solve the difference.

Walking a Mile in Her Shoes

1. **Empathy** is being able to see another person's thoughts, feelings, and point of view.

2. The mother of my children sees me as a _____ Dad. (Circle the answer.)

   Very Good   Good   Okay   Bad   Very Bad

3. She sees me this way because _____
   _____
   _____ .

SESSION 10 | Working with Mom and Co-Parenting

> She might never change her point of view and you might never agree with her point of view. However, seeing things from her point of view and understanding what you need to do to try and change it will help you be a better Dad and co-parent.

4. **Three things I can do to better see her point of view are:**

   1) _____
   _____

   2) _____
   _____

   3) _____
   _____

5. **Three things I can do to <u>try to change</u> her point of view are:**

   1) _____
   _____

   2) _____
   _____

   3) _____
   _____

6. She might never change her point of view and you might never agree with her point of view. However, seeing things from her point of view and understanding what you need to do to try and change it will help you be a better Dad and co-parent.

I'm Okay, She's Okay

1. **Same and Different as Parents Checklist**
   Rate yourself and the mother of your children based on your view, not what you think she would say. If you have children by more than one mother, think of the same mother as you did earlier during this session.
   1 = very low and 5 = very high. (Circle your answer.)

	Me	Her
Takes time for the children.	1 2 3 4 5	1 2 3 4 5
Listens to the children.	1 2 3 4 5	1 2 3 4 5
Respects the children's views.	1 2 3 4 5	1 2 3 4 5
Enjoys playing with the children.	1 2 3 4 5	1 2 3 4 5
Enforces the rules.	1 2 3 4 5	1 2 3 4 5
Is good with discipline.	1 2 3 4 5	1 2 3 4 5
Comforts the children when needed.	1 2 3 4 5	1 2 3 4 5
Is a good role model.	1 2 3 4 5	1 2 3 4 5
Respects the other parent in front of the children.	1 2 3 4 5	1 2 3 4 5
Has the children's respect.	1 2 3 4 5	1 2 3 4 5
Praises the children.	1 2 3 4 5	1 2 3 4 5
Shows anger in healthy ways.	1 2 3 4 5	1 2 3 4 5
Gives healthy touch to the children (hugs, kisses).	1 2 3 4 5	1 2 3 4 5
Tells the children to take healthy risks.	1 2 3 4 5	1 2 3 4 5
Builds self-worth in the children.	1 2 3 4 5	1 2 3 4 5

2. **For the Sake of the Children Tips:**
   - Your children will do better in life if they have the support of you and their mother.
   - Your children will have less stress if you and the mother value each other.
   - Don't talk badly about the mother in front of your children.
   - Don't talk with or confide in the children about a problem you have with the mother.
   - Tell your children often that they should love and respect their mother.
   - Tell your children that you love them even when you and the mother have problems with each other.
   - Never tell your children that they caused a problem between you and the mother.
   - Agree on how you will discipline the children before you discipline them.
   - Don't break an agreement between you and the mother without talking with her first.

What I Learned Log

1. One new thing I learned today is _____
   _____
   _____
   _____
   _____.

2. On a scale from 0 - 5, how likely am I to use what I learned?
   0 = Not at all likely   5 = Very likely

      0   1   2   3   4   5

3. What I learned will help me be a better dad because: _____

_____

_____

_____

_____ .

Notes

SESSION 11
Fathering from the Inside

Welcome and Warm-up

1. I contact my children _____
   (never, once a week, once a month, once every two months, etc.)

2. The main way I contact my children is by/to _____
   _____.

3. This amount of contact is _____
   _____.
   (about right, too little, too much)

Guidelines on Ways to Connect

1. You must commit to it—the way and the frequency.

2. It must be allowed by the prison/jail/facility.

3. It must be realistic given the likelihood of the caregiver of your children (mother, grandparent, etc.) allowing you to connect with your children in a specific way and how often you want to connect.

Get to Really Know Your Children

Knowing your children's likes, hopes, dreams, and fears will help you to have meaningful contact with your children. You will show an interest in your children. Your children will see and like that interest and know that you care about and love them. Knowing the milestones raises your awareness of the growth and challenges most children their age face and to be realistic about what your children should be able to do. A bonus is that your children's mother (or other caregiver) will also notice your interest and the care that shows. It might make her more willing to help you contact your children on a regular basis.

Fathering Plan
Ways I Will Connect with My Children

Ways I Will Connect

- What I do now:
  - ▶ Name of child _____

    How will I connect? _____
    _____
    _____

    How often will I connect? _____

  - ▶ Name of child _____

    How will I connect? _____
    _____
    _____

    How often will I connect? _____

  - ▶ Name of child _____

    How will I connect? _____
    _____
    _____

    How often will I connect? _____

  - ▶ Name of child _____

    How will I connect? _____
    _____
    _____

    How often will I connect? _____

SESSION 11 | Fathering from the Inside

- **What I will do/add:**

  ▶ Name of child _____

    How will I connect? _____
    _____
    _____

    How often will I connect? _____
    _____

  ▶ Name of child _____

    How will I connect? _____
    _____
    _____

    How often will I connect? _____
    _____

  ▶ Name of child _____

    How will I connect? _____
    _____
    _____

    How often will I connect? _____
    _____

  ▶ Name of child _____

    How will I connect? _____
    _____

    How often will I connect? _____
    _____

Fathering from the Inside | **SESSION 11**

What My Children Like

A MESSAGE FROM YOUR DAD

Because I love you and want to be the best father possible, I want to learn more about you. Please help me out by completing this worksheet and giving it back to me!

Love,
Your Dad

Name _____

Date _____ Age _____

Birthday _____
(month/date/year)

INFANTS / TODDLERS: AGE 0–3

YOUR FAVORITE:

Animal _____

Book _____

Cartoon _____

Cereal _____

Color _____

Drink _____

Flower _____

Friends _____

Fruit _____

Game _____

Holiday _____

Memory _____

Movie _____

Number _____

Part of School _____

Place to Eat _____

Teacher _____

Treat to Eat _____

Vegetable _____

SESSION 11 | Fathering from the Inside

A MESSAGE FROM YOUR DAD

Because I love you and want to be the best father possible, I want to learn more about you. Please help me out by completing this worksheet and giving it back to me!

Love,
Your Dad

Name _____

Date _____ Age _____

Birthday_____
(month/date/year)

Grade _____

PRESCHOOL / ELEMENTARY SCHOOL: AGE 4–12

YOUR FAVORITE:

Animal _____

Book _____

Cartoon _____

Cereal_____

Color_____

Drink _____

Flower _____

Friends _____

Fruit _____

Game _____

Holiday _____

Memory _____

Movie_____

Number _____

Part of School_____

Place to Eat_____

Teacher _____

Treat to Eat _____

Vegetable _____

SHARING MORE ABOUT YOU:

When I grow up, I want to be…

_____

Something I do not like:

_____

Something I am afraid of:

_____

I want to talk with you more about…

_____

_____

Something I would like to do with you soon is …

_____

_____

Something I would like to do with you when I get older is …

_____

_____

Another thing I want you to know is …

_____

_____

Fathering from the Inside | **SESSION 11**

A MESSAGE FROM YOUR DAD

Because I love you and want to be the best father possible, I want to learn more about you. Please help me out by completing this worksheet and giving it back to me!

*Love,
Your Dad*

Name _____

Date _____ Age _____

Birthday_____
(month/date/year)

Grade _____

MIDDLE / HIGH SCHOOL: AGE 13–18

YOUR FAVORITE:

Actor/Actress _____
Book _____
Cereal _____
Color _____
Food _____
Friends _____
_____
_____
Hobby _____
Holiday _____
Memory _____
Movie _____
Music _____
Pizza Topping_____
Place to Eat _____
School Subject _____
Sport _____
Sports Team _____
Store _____
Teacher _____
TV Show _____

Vacation Spot_____
Video Game _____
Website _____

SHARING MORE ABOUT YOU:

My dream job or career is … _____
_____

My worst fear is … _____
_____

Five things I can't stand are…
_____
_____
_____
_____
_____

Something I want to talk with my dad more about is …_____
_____
_____

Something I would like to do with my dad is …
_____
_____

SESSION 11 | Fathering from the Inside

What I Learned Log

1. One new thing I learned today is _____
   _____
   _____
   _____
   _____
   _____ .

2. On a scale from 0 - 5, how likely am I to use what I learned?
   0 = Not at all likely   5 = Very likely

       0   1   2   3   4   5

3. What I learned will help me be a better dad because: _____
   _____
   _____
   _____
   _____ .

Notes

_____
_____
_____
_____
_____
_____
_____

SESSION 12
Celebrate

Welcome and Warm-up

1. One change I've noticed in myself since the beginning of the program is _____
   _____
   _____
   _____
   _____ .

Skills I Learned

1. Five new fathering skills I have learned as a result of participating in this group are _____ ,
   _____ ,
   _____ ,
   _____ ,
   and _____ .

Celebrate

1. One thing I'm going to miss about this group is _____
   _____
   _____
   _____ .

2. When I think back to when we started, one thing I learned that will help me become a better dad is _____
   _____
   _____
   _____ .

SESSION 12 | Celebrate

Notes

Inside Out DAD®
Second Edition

APPENDIX
Ages & Stages

APPENDIX

1st & 2nd Months

With Contributions from Dr. Kyle Pruett and Dr. Yvette Warren.

Physical Growth	Mental/Emotional Growth	Social Growth
• Gains about 1/4 to 1/2 pound of weight each week for the first 6 months. • Height gain of about one inch each month. • Breaths mostly through nose. • Not able to hold head up in first month. Can turn head from side to side when lying on back. Lifts head by second month. • Body will be limp at knees and hips when held standing by parent. • When parent supports back, will round back by second month. Will also try to hold head up but will still bob forward. • In first month will keep hands closed tightly. By second month will often open hands and grasp.	• Watches object when held at a distance of 8–15 inches. By two months will follow toy from side to side. • Likes when people respond with their face (e.g. smile back at them). • Will quiet when hears parents' voice by two months. Knows familiar voices. • Cries during first month to show when hungry, wet, or uncomfortable.	• Closely watches parents' face when they play with him/her. • By second month can mimic parents' face (e.g. smiling and sticking out tongue).

Tips to Help Your Child Grow

1. Hold, cuddle, rock, talk, sing, hug, and kiss your baby often to make him/her feel safe.
2. Try to console and comfort your baby even though your baby might not always calm down.
3. If you can't spend a lot of time with your baby, play, talk, and sing during his alert stages (dressing, bathing, feeding, walking, driving) because it is more fun for you both.
4. Create routines and habits when you wash, feed, and put your baby to bed. Your baby will learn to rely on you and sleep better at night.
5. Use toys that are right for your baby's age.
6. Talk with your baby's doctor if you have any questions about how your baby is growing. Don't be afraid to talk about how you are doing as a dad.

3rd & 4th Months

With Contributions from Dr. Kyle Pruett and Dr. Yvette Warren.

Physical Growth

- More control of movement in neck, arms, legs, and chest.
- Soft spot on top of head still open. (Careful!)
- Drooling begins.
- Holds head straight up more often.
- Sits up straight if propped up.
- Raises head and chest up. Bears weight on forearms.
- Briefly supports some weight on legs if held up.
- Inspects and plays with own hands.
- Grasps and holds a rattle.
- Brings objects to mouth. (Careful!)
- Clutches at blankets or clothes.

Mental/Emotional Growth

- Locates sound by turning head and looking in same direction.
- Starts hand-eye coordination.
- Starts to cry less often. Cause of crying is easier to figure out.
- "Talks" a great deal when spoken to.
- Laughs, squeals, babbles, chuckles, and coos to show pleasure.

Social Growth

- Social smile begins to appear. Enjoy!
- Shows lots of interest in surroundings.
- Knows familiar faces and objects and shows pleasure.
- Seeks attention by making sounds, moving, and fussing. Stops crying when a familiar face enters the room.
- Begins to show memory of routines.
- Doesn't like too much stimulation or excitement.

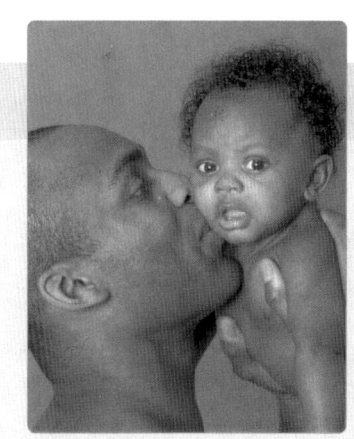

Tips to Help Your Child Grow

1. Hold, cuddle, rock, talk, sing, kiss, and hug your baby often to make him/her feel safe.
2. Talk and sing to your baby to help with making sounds. Repeat the sounds your baby "says" to you.
3. Read and play simple games with your baby.
4. Help your baby to console him or herself. Give your baby the same comfort object at bedtime or in new places. Your baby will choose one (blanket, stuffed animal, etc.) at some point. This makes your baby more independent in the long run.
5. Create a bedtime routine. Help your baby to console him/herself by putting him/her to bed awake after you help your baby quiet down.
6. Use toys that are right for your baby's age.

APPENDIX

5th & 6th Months

With Contributions from Dr. Kyle Pruett and Dr. Yvette Warren.

Physical Growth

- Birth weight has doubled.
- Growth rate slows.
- May only gain 3 to 5 ounces and grow 1/2 inch each month for the next 6 months.
- Brain tissue growing fast, but still fragile. Don't shake or play rough with your child.
- Gets lower center teeth.
- Able to sit for a longer time when back is well supported.
- Bears most of weight when held (briefly) standing by parent.
- Rolls from stomach to back. (Careful!)
- Puts feet to mouth.
- Sits in a high chair with back straight.
- Grasps objects on own.
- Takes objects straight to mouth.
- Holds bottle with both hands (briefly).

Mental/Emotional Growth

- Looks for a dropped object. May start a game.
- Looks for a long time at an object.
- Turns head to side and then look up or down.
- Squeals and coos in delight or excitement.

Social Growth

- Smiles at self in mirror.
- Pats bottle or breast with both hands.
- Starts more play.
- Holds up both arms to be picked up.
- Makes "upset" sounds when a familiar object or person is taken away /leaves.
- Mimics what hears (cough, tongue noises, etc.).
- Changes emotions often.

Tips to Help Your Child Grow

1. Help your baby to talk by copying sounds she/he enjoys making.
2. Read to your baby and play music (of all kinds).
3. Play social games (patty cake, peek-a-boo, hide and seek with people/objects).
4. Use toys that are right for your baby's age.
5. Set limits on behavior (throwing) at this age using distraction, control of surroundings (e.g. lights not too bright and no loud noises), structure, and routine. Too early to use discipline.
6. Keep up bathing, feeding, and bedtime routines and other habits to keep your baby from getting tired and waking up at night.
7. Help your baby learn to console him/herself by putting your child to bed awake.

7th & 8th Months

With Contributions from Dr. Kyle Pruett and Dr. Yvette Warren.

Physical Growth

- Gets upper center teeth.
- Shows a pattern in peeing and pooping.
- Sits leaning forward on both hands.
- Bears full weight on feet when standing and bounces.
- Moves objects from one hand to the other.
- Bangs objects together.
- Rakes with fingers at small objects.
- Begins to grasp small objects with fingers. (Careful! Can choke on small objects put in mouth.)
- Lets go of object at will (or not).
- Reaches for toys out of reach.

Mental/Emotional Growth

- Responds to own name.
- Turns head toward sounds with a smile or frown. Looks at the people or things that make sounds.
- Starts to like or dislike foods with certain tastes.
- Makes vowel sounds and what sounds like words (baba, dada, kiki) but does not know what they mean.

Social Growth

- Is aware of adults who are not his/her parents. More aware of and might have a fear of strangers.
- Mimics simple acts and noises.
- Coughs or snorts to draw attention to self.
- Keeps lips closed to show dislike of some foods.
- Might bite to show excitement or aggression.
- Looks briefly for toys that go out of sight.
- Starts response to word "no."

Tips to Help Your Child Grow

1. Help your baby to talk by talking to him/her and using his/her new sounds.
2. Increase your baby's social circle and involve your baby in your social things. Don't let too many strangers handle your child.
3. Read and sing to your baby and play music (of all kinds).
4. Play games (patty cake, peek-a-boo, tickle bee, etc).
5. Use toys that are right for your baby's age.
6. Keep small objects out of reach because your baby can choke on them.
7. To set limits for your baby, use distraction, stimulus control, structure, and routine.
8. Limit the number of rules and always enforce them.
9. Maintain the bedtime routine. Help your baby learn to console him/herself by putting him/her to bed awake.

APPENDIX

9th & 10th Months

With Contributions from Dr. Kyle Pruett and Dr. Yvette Warren.

Physical Growth

- More teeth come in and might cause pain.
- Raises head while lying down or when sitting.
- Starts to crawl. Might crawl backward at first. Will pull self forward. (Careful!)
- Pushes up from lying to sitting on own.
- Sits on floor for longer amounts of time.
- Pulls up and stands holding onto furniture.
- Uses thumb and index finger to grasp small objects.
- Might start to show whether left or right-handed.

Mental/Emotional Growth

- Better able to judge distance (as between objects and people) but not height (as in how tall something is or how far from a chair to the ground).
- Turns head toward sound.
- Responds to simple commands.
- Says "dada" and "mama" and starts to know what those words mean.
- Mimics real speech.
- Speaks gibberish. Sounds like a sentence but isn't yet.
- May fear going to bed or being left alone.

Social Growth

- Parents important for play and comfort.
- Wants to please parents a lot.
- Puts arm in front of face to avoid being washed.
- Mimics looks on people's faces (frowns, smiles, etc.).
- Likes attention. Repeats actions or pulls at clothes for attention.
- Cries when scolded or scared.
- Starts to show independence in dressing, feeding, and testing parents.

Tips to Help Your Child Grow

1. Your baby is in motion so baby proof your home to keep your baby from getting hurt.
2. Provide an area where your baby can explore and practice new skills.
3. Talk with your baby and respond to his/her vocal efforts.
4. Read to and sing to your baby and play music (of all kinds).
5. Play social games (patty cake, peek-a-boo, etc.).
6. Use toys that are right for your baby's age.
7. To set limits on aggression and discipline, use distraction, stimulus control, structure, and routine.
8. Limit the number of rules and always enforce them.
9. Maintain a bedtime routine.

11th & 12th Months

With Contributions from Dr. Kyle Pruett and Dr. Yvette Warren.

Physical Growth

- More teeth come in.
- Birth weight has about tripled and birth height has doubled.
- Soft spot on head is almost closed.
- Crawls well.
- Walks holding onto furniture or your hand.
- Can sit down from standing.
- When sitting, turns to reach backward to pick up an object.
- Holds a crayon.
- Explores objects more closely. (Still uses mouth—careful!)
- Drops objects into a box, bowl, cup, etc.
- Can turn pages in a book often many at a time

Mental/Emotional Growth

- Can follow objects that move fast.
- Knows meaning of hundreds of words even though may only speak two or three words.
- Knows objects by name.
- Knows simple commands.

Social Growth

- Feels joy and self-esteem when masters a task.
- May get frustrated or angry when kept from doing something.
- Shows emotions of all kinds.
- Fears strange places or settings.
- May further develop habits with comfort objects like a blanket.

Tips to Help Your Child Grow

1. Praise your baby for doing good and learning new skills and knowledge.
2. Help your baby to talk by reading books, singing, and talking about what you do and see. Use books with stiff pages (like cardboard) that your baby can turn by him/herself.
3. Help your baby to follow simple commands by playing a game where he/she points to the right body part when you say "Where is your eye?; Where is your nose?;" etc.
4. Help your baby to **safely** explore and take risks.
5. Allow your baby to play by him or herself for a short time while you watch. But never leave your child out of your sight.
6. To set limits, use distraction and gentle restraint. Take objects away and use time out if needed.
7. Limit number of rules and use structure. Head off trouble before it starts to prevent conflict.
8. Maintain a bedtime routine to help your baby sleep through the night.
9. Your baby probably is not ready to potty train. Feel free to talk with your baby's doctor about when to start.
10. Limit the amount of TV your baby watches, even "educational TV." It is not nearly as good as time spent with you.

1st & 2nd Years

With Contributions from Dr. Kyle Pruett and Dr. Yvette Warren.

Physical Growth

- Weight gain is about 4 to 6 pounds per year.
- Growth is about 4 to 5 inches per year.
- May have daytime poop/bowel control.
- Walks without help.
- Very mobile. Starts to climb stairs, at first by creeping and then with two feet on each step.
- Learns to run, at first falling often.
- As he/she gains more balance, stands without help.
- Stops quickly without falling. Picks up objects and kicks and throws a ball.
- Likes to push and pull toys.
- Seats self in chair.
- Uses a cup.
- Scribbles on own.
- Builds a tower of 6 or 7 blocks.
- Turns doorknob and unscrews lids.

Mental/Emotional Growth

- Names some shapes.
- Shows intense like for pictures.
- Able to speak about 300 words by the end of second year.
- Knows 1 or 2 direct commands.
- Refers to self by name.
- Often talks all the time.

Social Growth

- Okay being apart from parent sometimes.
- Shows emotions. Hugs and kisses parents and has temper tantrums.
- Opens drawers and doors to find objects.
- Mimics both good and bad behavior very well.
- Starts to know he/she "owns" some things.
- Has some sense of time. Waits when told "wait a minute."
- Able to undress self before dresses self. Then able to dress self in simple clothes.

APPENDIX

With Contributions from Dr. Kyle Pruett and Dr. Yvette Warren.

Tips to Help Your Child Grow

1. Praise your child for doing good and learning new skills and knowledge.

2. Help your child to talk by reading books, singing, and talking about what you do and see. Point out colors, shapes, and letters.

3. Support your child's attempts to care for and express him/herself.

4. Help your child to make simple choices as often as you can.

5. Help your child to assert him/herself in the right settings.

6. Decide on the best limits for your child and start to discipline. Briefly tell your child why she/he is being disciplined. Enforce limits and keep discipline short and simple.

7. Focus discipline on the "action" and not the "actor." ("I love you, but I don't like it when you…")

8. Try to give your child a "yes" and a "no" when you discipline. ("You can't play with the vase. You can play with the blocks.")

9. Don't get into a power struggle with your child. Avoid conflict and use your power calmly and swiftly. You can control only how you react to what your child says and does. You can't make your child sleep, for example, but you can insist your child stays in his/her room.

10. Delay potty training until your child keeps a dry diaper for about two hours, knows when he/she is wet and dry, can pull pants up, wants to learn, and gives a signal when about to poop.

11. Spend time alone with your child. This is really important if you have other children. Play with, hug, and hold your child. Take walks, paint, and do puzzles together.

12. Allow your child to explore and take risks in the right settings. Don't limit too much.

13. Promote safe physical activity.

14. Help your child play with other children, but don't expect your child to share yet.

15. Use time out or remove the source of conflict (like a toy) for doing bad things.

16. Figure out how you will deal with your child waking at night and having night fears and nightmares.

17. Limit the amount of TV your child watches, even "educational TV." It is not nearly as good as time spent with you.

APPENDIX

3rd Year

With Contributions from Dr. Kyle Pruett and Dr. Yvette Warren.

Physical Growth

- Gains about 4 to 6 pounds and grows about 3 inches.
- Will sometimes get through the night without having to pee or poop.
- Rides/peddles a tricycle.
- Jumps off bottom stair.
- Stands on one foot.
- Uses one foot and then the other when going up from stair to stair.
- Tries to dance.
- Draws circles and crosses.
- Builds towers and bridges with blocks.

Mental/Emotional Growth

- Speaks about 900 words.
- Uses complete sentences with three or four words.
- May talk all the time.
- Can dress almost all by self.
- Feeds self.
- Helps with simple one or two-step tasks.
- May have fear of dark or going to bed.
- Talks to dolls, animals, trucks, etc.

Social Growth

- Still selfish in thought and behavior, but can start to see things from others' point of view.
- Often tries to please parents and say and do what they expect
- Is aware of family relationships and sex roles.
- Boys start to see that they are like their father and other men in the family. Girls start to see that they are like their mother and other women in the family.
- Starts to use play to be social with others.
- Better able to share and wait turn.

Tips to Help Your Child Grow

1. Praise your child for doing good and learning new skills and knowledge.
2. Ask your child to talk with you about the good and bad things with his/her preschool, friends, and what he/she sees going on around him/her. Ask simple questions that don't require judgment.
3. Read to and with your child. Be patient because he/she might repeat words a lot and more than you would like!
4. Spend alone time with your child. This is really important if you have other children.
5. Create times for your child to play and hang out with other children.
6. Delay potty training until your child keeps a dry diaper for about two hours, knows when he/she is wet and dry, can pull pants up, wants to learn, and gives a signal when he/she is about to poop. It's okay to wait to potty train a three-year old if he/she isn't ready. Talk with your child's doctor if you are worried that your child isn't ready.
7. Promote safe physical activity.
8. Remind your child of and enforce limits and the right behavior.
9. Give your child chances to make choices.
10. Limit TV to about an hour a day of good, non-adult programs that teach/educate. Watch with your child. Don't let your child watch TV alone.

APPENDIX

4th Year

With Contributions from Dr. Kyle Pruett and Dr. Yvette Warren.

Physical Growth

- Gains about 4 to 6 pounds and grows about 3 inches.
- Skips and hops on one foot.
- Catches and throws a ball.
- Uses scissors well.
- Draws squares and stick figures.

Mental/Emotional Growth

- Speaks about 1500 words.
- Uses complete sentences with three or four words.
- Talks all the time.
- Asks a lot of questions.
- Tells "tall" or "make-believe" stories.
- Knows simple songs.
- Knows meaning of "under," "on top of," "beside," "in back" or "in front of."
- Can repeat four digits /numbers.
- Often loves to help cook, clean, put laundry away.
- Still has many fears (thunder, dogs, etc.).
- Knows time better (as in when events like bedtime and lunch happen during the day).
- May count but knows little or no math.
- Do's and don'ts become important.

Social Growth

- Quite independent.
- Still selfish, impatient, and aggressive.
- Boasts, tattles, and tells stories about family.
- Make-believe friends are common.
- Works through conflict with some help.
- Takes anger and frustration out on parents and siblings.

Tips to Help Your Child Grow

1. Praise your child for doing good and learning new skills and knowledge.
2. Ask your child to talk with you about the good and bad things with his/her preschool, friends, and what he/she sees going on around him/her. Answer questions.
3. Read to and with your child.
4. Spend alone time with your child. This is very important if you have other children.
5. Create times for your child to play and hang out with other children.
6. Promote safe physical activity.
7. Remind your child of and enforce limits and the right behavior.
8. Give your child chances to make choices, create things, and do nice, giving things for family and others.
9. Limit TV to about an hour a day of good, non-adult programs that teach/educate. Watch with your child. Don't let your child watch TV alone.
10. Help your child to assert him/herself without being aggressive.
11. Put your child in new settings/places and keep letting him/her take safe risks.

APPENDIX

5th Year

With Contributions from Dr. Kyle Pruett and Dr. Yvette Warren.

Physical Growth	Mental/Emotional Growth	Social Growth
• Grows 2-3 inches but gains as little as 2-4 pounds a year. Children grow and gain weight at very different rates. • May start to get adult teeth. • Clearly right or left-handed. • Skips and hops on one foot and then the other. • Catches and throws a ball. • Jumps rope and skates. • Learns to tie shoes.	• Speaks about 2500 words. • Uses complete sentences with many words. • Learns to name coins, colors, days of week, months. • Asks meaning of words. • Asks thoughtful questions. • Takes basic care of self (dress, brush teeth). • Writes a few letters, numbers, and words. • Helps with simple chores.	• More settled and focused when with others. • More independent and trustworthy. • Relies on others (parents) to control their world. • Likes rules and tries to play by them but may cheat to avoid losing. • Begins to notice the outside world and where/how belongs. • Enjoys doing things with parent of same sex.

Tips to Help Your Child Grow

1. Praise your child for cooperation and learning new skills and knowledge.
2. Ask your child to talk with you about his/her world (school and friends). Prime the pump by telling him/her a little about yours.
3. Tell your child to show feelings. This is very important with boys.
4. Read to and with your child.
5. Spend alone time with your child doing something you both enjoy. This is really important if you have other children.
6. Put your child in new settings and keep letting him/her take safe risks. Take on something new for **both** of you.
7. Create times for your child to play and hang out with other children.
8. Help your child learn to get along with peers. Role model how to get along with others.
9. Promote safe physical activity and keep a limit on watching TV and computer use.
10. Give chores that are right for your child's age. Don't pay them (an allowance) for doing chores.
11. Show how to use a computer.
12. Expect your child to follow rules, such as those for bedtime, TV, computer, and chores.
13. Teach your child the difference between right and wrong, to respect others/people in charge, and how to manage anger.

6th & 7th Year

With Contributions from Dr. Kyle Pruett and Dr. Yvette Warren.

Physical Growth

- Height and weight gain is slow. Grows about 2 inches and 5 pounds a year.
- Wisdom teeth start to come in.
- Still uses fingers when eating.
- Practices new skills.
- Draws, writes, and colors.
- Uses knife to spread butter or jam.
- Cuts, folds, pastes paper.
- Makes simple figures in clay or Play-doh®.

Mental/Emotional Growth

- Uses new language, memory, and math skills.
- Counts up to 13 pennies.
- Knows whether it is morning or afternoon.
- Defines common objects such as "fork" and "chair" in terms of use.
- Follows three commands when given at once.
- Says which is pretty and which is ugly when looking at pictures.
- Reads from memory and enjoys oral spelling games.
- Likes table games, checkers, and simple card games.
- Has own way of doing things.
- Tries skills on own.
- Often frustrated.
- Has hard time owning up to doing wrong.
- Sometimes steals money or objects and then lies.
- Takes a bath without being watched. Does bedtime routine alone.

Social Growth

- Shares and cooperates better.
- Has strong need for play with peers.
- Often plays rough.
- Often jealous of younger siblings.
- Does what sees adults do whether good or bad.
- Likes to boast.
- Might cheat to win.
- Influenced by friends.

Tips to Help Your Child Grow

1. Praise your child for cooperation and learning new skills and knowledge.
2. Ask your child to talk about his/her world (school and friends). Listen carefully and remember what he/she says. Answer your child's questions.
3. Tell your child to show feelings. Role model by showing yours. This is very important for boys.
4. Read to and with your child. Tell your child to read alone.
5. Spend alone time with your child doing something both of you enjoy. This is really important if you have other children.
6. Expand your child's world through family trips and outings.
7. Help your child learn how to get along with peers.
8. Help your child learn how to follow group rules.
9. Promote daily, safe physical activity. Watch TV habits and limit amount of TV and computer use.

—continued

APPENDIX

With Contributions from Dr. Kyle Pruett and Dr. Yvette Warren.

6th & 7th Year: Tips to Help Your Child Grow—continued

10. Set limits and clear rules for discipline and punishment for bad behavior.
11. Help your child to discipline him/herself and to control impulses.
12. Expect your child to follow family rules, such as those at bedtime, TV watching, and doing chores. Don't pay your child (an allowance) for chores.
13. Teach your child to respect others/people in charge.
14. Help your child's ability to communicate with you, teachers, and other adults by going to school.
15. Tell your child often the difference between right and wrong.
16. Teach your child how to manage anger and resolve conflicts without physical or emotional violence.

8th & 9th Year

With Contributions from Dr. Kyle Pruett and Dr. Yvette Warren.

Physical Growth	Mental/Emotional Growth	Social Growth
• Grows about 2 inches and gains about 6 pounds a year. • Always on the go. Jumps, chases, and skips. • Greater smoothness and speed in motor control. • Movement fluid, often graceful and poised. • Eyes and hands are well coordinated.	• Can use common tools such as a hammer, blender, egg beater, and toaster as long as parent watches them. Don't allow to use tools alone. • Helps with household tasks. • Looks after all of own needs at table. • Shows some choice in buying things. • Great reader. Likes magazines with lots of pictures. • Likes school. • Likely to overdo things. Hard to quiet down after recess. • Dresses self on own and often with same type of clothing. • Says what is alike and different about two things from memory. • Repeats days of the week and months in order. • Counts backward from 20. • Makes change out of a quarter. • Likes rewards. • Reads classic books and enjoys comics. • Harder on self. • Knows right from wrong. Starts to understand fairness. • More aware of time. Gets to school on time. • Afraid of failing a grade. Ashamed of bad grades, mistakes.	• Easy to get along with at home and better behaved. • Often shows off. • Relates more easily to others. • Interested in boy-girl relationships but will not admit it. • Likes to compete and play games.

Tips to Help Your Child Grow

1. Role model morals, values, ethics, and behavior.
2. Help with your child's self-esteem by honoring his/her effort and showing you love him/her.
3. Show and tell your child how important school is. Go to parent-teacher meetings and other school events. Learn about school projects and help with homework because there is more of it and it's harder.
4. Be fair with what you expect from your child. Challenge your child to set high but fair goals.
5. Promote a sense of responsibility for his/her actions.
6. Role model affection and respect for family.
7. Spend alone time with your child. This is very important if you have other children.
8. Promote safe, physical activity and set a limit on watching TV and computer use.
9. Share meals as a family. Ask your child to help prepare meals.
10. Know your child's friends and their families.
11. Handle anger well in the family.
12. Set aside special time just to talk with your child.
13. Teach your child how to manage anger and resolve conflicts without physical or emotional violence.

APPENDIX

10th & 11th Year

With Contributions from Dr. Kyle Pruett and Dr. Yvette Warren.

Physical Growth

- Slow growth in height but rapid weight gain. May become obese/heavy during this time if not active.
- Posture more similar to an adult's.
- May start puberty. Body lines in girls soften and round out.
- Rest of adult teeth come in.

Mental/Emotional Growth

- May do work on own around home (chores) and neighborhood.
- Meets own needs or those of other children left briefly in his/her care.
- Cooks, sews, repairs things, cares for pets, and does other "adult" tasks when learns them.
- Washes and dries own hair but may need reminding.
- Starts to do more homework without help from parents.
- Uses phone and computer more often.
- Reads more for pleasure and to learn (magazines, books, websites).
- Knows more than just what is right and wrong. Can explain the morals and values that make something right or wrong.

Social Growth

- Likes family. Family has more meaning.
- Likes mother and wants to please her.
- More comfort with showing affection (hugs) to non-family.
- Adores and looks up to father. (Enjoy it while it lasts!)
- Likes friends and talks about them all the time.
- More "choosey" with friends.
- Starts to like the other sex.
- Is more polite to others, shrewd, and clever.
- Writes short letters and e-mails to friends and family.

Tips to Help Your Child Grow

1. Be ready for a lot of new behavior ahead of the teen years. Friends become more important. Your child might talk back to you more often and test you in other ways. He/she will try to be more independent such as refuse to take part in family events. He/she may be more moody and take new, unsafe risks.
2. Role model morals, values, ethics, and behavior. Your child watches you more closely than ever.
3. Help your child's self-esteem by praising him/her and showing you love him/her.
4. Show and tell your child how important school is. Go to parent-teacher meetings and other school events. Learn about school projects and help with homework because there is more of it and it's harder.
5. Be fair with what you expect from your child. Challenge your child to set high but fair goals.
6. Promote a sense of responsibility for own actions at and away from home.
7. Promote safe, physical activity and set a limit on watching TV and computer use.
8. Share meals as a family.
9. Know your child's friends and their families.
10. Set aside time just to talk with your child.
11. Discuss and show the value and meaning of money in family and culture. Discuss an allowance, chores, savings, gift giving, charity, etc.
12. Teach your child how to manage anger and resolve conflicts without physical or emotional violence.

12th – 14th Years

With Contributions from Dr. Kyle Pruett and Dr. Yvette Warren.

Physical Growth

- Lots of growth in weight and height. Gain in height is rapid for first two years and then slows down.
- Likely to get acne.
- Girls are ahead of boys in growth by about two years.
- Puberty starts early for some and later for others. It might not start until 15 or 16.
- Boys have "wet dreams."
- Better coordinated, but boys may appear awkward at times. (Look like they need to "grow into their body.")
- Struggles to master new physical skills.

Mental/Emotional Growth

- Starts to think about culture, politics, religion, death, and other life issues.
- Tries out different roles, and explores "who they are."
- Becomes more private with being naked (girls in front of dad and boys in front of mom).
- Better able to do homework without help from parents. May rely more on peers for help with homework.
- Peers' views of how he/she looks affects view of him/herself (body image).
- Likes watching TV, listening to music, talking on the phone/Internet, sports, and group activities.
- Anxious about how he/she looks and changing body. May be very concerned about being small.
- Anxious about place in the world.

Social Growth

- Compares being normal with peers of same sex.
- Creates close friendships with members of same sex.
- Uses humor to criticize family and friends.
- Struggles with being part of a group (dress and ways of talking) while being themselves.
- Can still be very selfish.
- Boys often discuss sports, sports figures, and video games with each other.
- Girls often discuss boys, clothes, and makeup with each other.

—continued

12th – 14th Years: Tips to Help Your Child Grow—continued

1. Be ready for teen behavior. Friends become more important. Your child might talk back to you more often and test you in other ways. He/she will try to be more independent such as refuse to take part in family events. He/she may be more moody and take new, unsafe risks.

2. Decide with your child when he/she can do things on his/her own, including staying at home alone.

3. Be fair with what you expect from your child. Give your child more independence and responsibility as he/she can handle and earns it.

4. Set clear limits and discipline and punishment for breaking rules. Use humor to get your point across.

5. Show and tell your child how important school is. Go to parent-teacher meetings and school events. Help with homework because there is more of it and it's harder. Suggest that peers help with homework (study groups).

6. Help your child's self-esteem by praising him/her often and showing you love him/her. Don't criticize a lot, nag, or make fun of your child.

7. Set aside time just to talk and do other things with your child, even if he/she doesn't ask for it.

8. Respect your child's need for privacy—both physical and emotional.

9. Tell your child what you expect with regard to drug and alcohol use and dating now and in the future.

10. Teach your child how to manage anger and resolve conflicts without physical or emotional violence.

11. Closely watch TV viewing habits. Your child might start to like adult programs, so be careful. A lot of "teen" shows have adult themes.

15 – 17th Years

With Contributions from Dr. Kyle Pruett and Dr. Yvette Warren.

Physical Growth	Mental/Emotional Growth	Social Growth
• Girls stop growing. Boys keep growing and start to "fill out." • May think about or masturbate often.	• More abstract (not concrete) thinking. • Uses logic and debates an issue. • Starts to know that others' thoughts don't always have to do with them. • Private with being naked. Doesn't like parents or siblings to see naked. • Worries about school work. • Does almost all homework without help from parents. Relies more on peers for help with homework. • Likes using "smarts" and outwitting others. • May fall in love and learn about "being in love." • Explores "sex appeal." May wear "revealing" clothes. • May want a car for freedom. • Has or wants a job to earn money. • May try alcohol or drugs. • Wants to learn and discover things on own. Wants more freedom. • Tries to see how he/she looks (body image) through his/her own eyes more than through peers' views. • Often sees and may talk about own flaws and how he/she fails at things. Has a hard time asking for help. Often detaches from emotions and feelings. • Tends to withdraw when upset or hurt.	• Can still be very selfish. More "arrogant" or "full of" him/herself. • Relationship with parents may be at a low point. • Greater push for freedom can cause conflict in relationships. • Being liked by peers is very important. Big fear of rejection/not being liked.

Tips to Help Your Child Grow

1. Be ready for teen behavior. Friends are very important. Your child will talk back to you more often and test you in other ways. He/she will try to be more independent such as refuse to take part in family events. He/she may be more moody and take new, unsafe risks.
2. Decide with your child when he/she can do things on his/her own, including staying at home alone.
3. Be fair with what you expect from your child. Give your child more independence and responsibility as he/she can handle and earns it.
4. Set clear limits and discipline and punishment for breaking rules. Use humor to get your point across.
5. Show and tell your child how important school is. Go to school events. Help with homework because there is more of it and it is harder. Suggest that peers help with homework (study groups).
6. Help your child's self-esteem by praising him/her often and showing you love him/her. Don't criticize a lot, nag, or make fun of your child.
7. Set aside time to spend with your child even if he/she doesn't ask for it.
8. Respect your child's need for privacy—both physical and emotional.
9. Tell your child what you expect with regard to drug and alcohol use and dating now and in the future.
10. Teach your child how to manage anger and resolve conflicts without physical or emotional violence.

APPENDIX

18th Year & Up

With Contributions from Dr. Kyle Pruett and Dr. Yvette Warren.

Physical Growth	Mental/Emotional Growth	Social Growth
• Boys stop growing with growth in height stopping at 18 to 20 years. • Feels better about physical growth.	• Better able to follow morals and values when faces challenge. • Able to view complex problems with an open mind and less personally. • Links goals to action. • Life goals and tasks take shape. • Pursues a career and decides how will live life. • Emotions more stable and easy to predict. • Better at hiding anger and frustration. • Who he/she is takes form. • More self-esteem. • Sees body image more through own eyes than based on peers' views.	• Begins to think more about a long-term relationship with a member of the other sex. • Has fewer conflicts with family. • Greater freedom from family. • Takes or leaves advice. • Forms stable relationships and stronger, deeper ties to others. • Peer groups less important. • Less selfish in relationships.

Tips to Help Your Child Grow

1. This time can be very hard on you and your child as he/she moves away from home. Be ready for your child to take more risks now that he/she is out of the house and be there for your child if needed.
2. Tell your child to make own decisions as often as he/she can.
3. Talk often about plans for the future, such as living away from home, college, career, family, and money.
4. If your child still lives at home, create family rules that you and he/she agree to follow. Your relationship becomes more adult to adult than adult to child.
5. Help your child's self-esteem by praising him/her often and showing you love him/her. Don't criticize a lot, nag, or make fun of your child.
6. Set aside time to spend with your child even if he/she doesn't ask for it or live with you. If your child lives in another town or city, set aside time to talk over the phone or through e-mail/online.
7. Even though your child might be in college, keep stressing how important school is to success in life.
8. Respect your child's need for privacy—both physical and emotional.
9. Teach your child how to manage anger and resolve conflicts without physical or emotional violence.